MORE PRAISE FOR
LESSONS FROM THE GARDEN

Kate Dahlstedt's *Lessons from the Garden* will cause you to narrow your focus, down and down again, to the everyday, yet defining and intimate moments of a human life. The work is bookended by two thoughtful essays, "Lessons from the Garden," and "Meditation on Trees" which extrapolate the seasons of gardens and trees, to the milestones and patterns of our existence. The space in between is filled in with spare, wise and poignant poetry that seems to skip the brain and penetrate the heart.

~Susan Raby-Dunne, Canadian author, military historian and battlefield guide

Poems offer us life at an oblique angle. Kate's series of angles include: Love, Mothering, War, Loss and Spirit. In each terrain this fine poet reveals the joy of life in sorrow and the sorrows of life through joy. The space in which she creates these deeply meditative poems is that thin arena between darkness and light. What a treat the reader has in store!

~Dennis Patrick Slattery, Ph.D, author of *Just Below the Water Line: Selected Poems; Twisted Sky: Selected Poems;* and *Leaves From the World Tree: Selected Poems,* with Craig Deininger

LESSONS FROM THE GARDEN

Selected Poems and Essays

by

Kate Dahlstedt

978-1-950186-23-5

Cover Photograph by Lee Seonghak
Author Photo (2020) by Edward Tick
Cover Design by Jennifer Leigh Selig

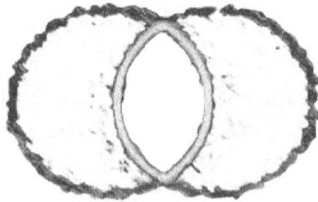

MANDORLA BOOKS
WWW.MANDORLABOOKS.COM

This book is dedicated to my family whose stories are woven throughout these pages, my husband and chief supporter Ed and our two children Gabriel and Sappho. Our lives together are my greatest treasure.

CONTENTS

WAR

LOSS

SPIRIT

INTRODUCTION

Lessons from the Garden is a memoir, a glimpse of the rhythm and rhyme of my life through time. Some of the poems go back 40 years, from courtship to becoming a wife, stepmother and mother. Others evolved from my Hospice social work with dying patients as well as my work with military veterans. Mostly, they are reflections on the everyday, ordinary events of life, in a way that gives them greater meaning.

The title refers, of course, to the metaphors all around us, as many of my poems do. Poetry requires that the reader be able to imagine the experience, to feel it in their own hearts and bodies, to sense it through the meter, music, repeated sounds and the use of universal language, resonant imagery and metaphor that focuses us on the actual while at the same time revealing the hidden. I have been called a lyric poet. My "muse" insists on the "music" of a piece, whether it's through sound, rhythm or symbolism.

Primarily though, these pages reveal my reverent awareness of the "great Web of Life" that connects us and all else.

LESSONS FROM THE GARDEN

A tiny purple weed leaning toward a crack of sunlight, a pair of mourning doves taking turns at the feeder, rainwater caught in the fold of a leaf, tiny miracles surround us. If we pause to notice, they offer us a host of wisdom.

Gardening books and articles help us create and improve our natural spaces, but seldom are we encouraged to reflect on the life lessons that abound in the everyday garden. Spring comes...finally... and without fail life overflows. Spend an afternoon in a backyard garden watching the wonders there and you will see an amazing reflection of the larger world around us. Notice the little things. Here are just a few.

Flower gardening begins with inspiration. The gardener envisions the natural space in much the same way an artist imagines a canvas. Whether they are looking at the whole yard or just a corner, gardeners seek to create beauty using the earth's natural bounty. As with any act of creating, especially utilizing nature, gardening can engender a sense of joining with universal creative forces. Sitting in the garden, we know in our bones that the natural world—the wonder and the mystery—is an ever-flowing stream, reliable and true. And when we immerse ourselves in that abundance, we can begin to feel a grand design and our own place in it.

One of the most essential things a gardener has to do is become acquainted with the critters that naturally inhabit the territory, the birds, bugs, weeds and wildflowers. We discover how the players behave, who needs what, and how we want to respond. It may take a few years of observation, but eventually patterns begin to emerge.

We watch over our gardens as a mother might tend to her children, keeping their needs in mind while encouraging them to grow into themselves. We protect tiny shoots from too much sun and make sure everybody has enough water. We give them healthy food to encourage their growth and worry when they seem sick. We do in our gardens what we do with family and friends.

Gardening also lets us indulge, to create what we love by adapting the environment. Encouraging bird life may mean growing some berries or adding a water source. Weeds that fill in bare spots may have pretty blooms that can be incorporated into the landscape rather than simply being yanked.

When we watch closely, we see that even the smallest of creatures has an interesting life, however brief, and that each one has a purpose, if only to be food for another. We gain an appreciation for ourselves as humans, and our place in the natural order. And we are reminded that beauty and value come in many forms.

In the web of human relations, we never know what impact the tiniest act might have on others. We don't always see the ripples. A natural gardener needs to keep an open mind and not be quick to judge. Sitting in the garden, we learn to respect others, no matter their social status, as being an important thread in the larger social fabric.

One thing gardeners know is that living things will compete for resources and that some living things are more aggressive than others. These are known as invasive species and if left unchecked they will crowd out other species and take over empty spaces. It is hard not to think of them as little soldiers "taking ground" from a helpless enemy. Rather than simply killing the unwanted plants with poisonous chemicals, the experienced gardener has to be like a political diplomat and learn to prevent invasions.

We must discourage a takeover by doing such things as planting other hardy species that will dig in roots and not be easily taken over, planting to create more shade, or pruning to make way for more sunlight. In other words, diversity and flexibility are necessary to sustain a vibrant living whole. There is enough to go around if distributed fairly. Perhaps we humans could learn to live in harmony with each other, for the benefit of all, like the green things in our gardens.

Some gardeners are very strict about what can grow where, while others are a little more liberal. One person's weed is another person's wildflower. But, unless you want a jungle, you will likely have to decide at some point what to pull, what to mow down, and what to leave alone. A garden, like life, is an ever-evolving creation. When something grows out of place or too big the gardener must act to pluck or to prune out excess. This is true of our lives as well. Some things we enjoy and commit to at one time in our lives may not serve us as well in another. Learning to say no to what we don't want or need, cleaning out our excess, simplifies our lives and makes new growth possible.

Gardeners know that if you want to transplant or get rid of a plant or weeds you must dig down to the roots and pull them out. Otherwise they are likely to keep growing back and disrupting things. It is the same with our feelings. When we bury our painful emotions such as sadness, anger, resentment, they don't go away. Rather they stay deep inside, sapping our energy and tainting how we view the world. Like the plants, we need to dig down to the root of the feelings, the original hurts, in order to heal them and stop them from hurting us more.

Another fascinating lesson about roots is that some plants can grow new ones when the original ones are severed. All they need is the right medium. Sometimes just the end of a leaf or bare stem can be placed in a jar of water and within days, new roots begin to form. The lesson for us is that even when we are devastated by fundamental loss, be it a loved one, a job, a home, a marriage, it is still possible to grow new, strong roots that will continue to sustain us. In the face of great loss there is hope.

Gardening reminds us that life's unpredictability is as much a natural fact as it's predictability. The sun rises and sets every day, but we are never quite sure where those pesky weeds will pop up or how many blooms the peonies will yield. Despite all our efforts and calculations, we are sometimes delighted by a surprise sprouting in the perfect place or saddened by what did not return from last year. We learn that we can only have minimal control and that forces other than our own are always at play. In the end we have to go with the flow of what is and make the best of it.

Many gardeners find that some corners or out of the way space in their yards are just best left alone. Tall grasses mix with ferns and runaway phlox. It could be neater, it could be thinned, it could be transplanted. But there is something primally appealing about leaving a little wildness, some unrestricted place that reminds us to lighten up, that gives us permission to kick back sometimes and just be our natural, unkempt, wonderfully fertile selves.

A gardener has to be patient. Nature has its own rhythm. It is not up to us when the blooms will open. We plant and nurture and tend, but ultimately, we must wait. Time, soil, sunlight and something else, something unknowable, do the rest. In the end we must surrender to them all. And with our surrender we develop faith. Though we don't know exactly when or where, we are sure that something magical, something wondrous, will always happen in the garden.

LOVE

Love

Time after time
you come back to me
in the center
back and beyond back
to where we are
anew.

Time after time
you are waiting there for me
arms out wide
and me out of breath from wandering
running to them
as if the first time.

Time after time
we dare to peer into the landscape
of each other's eyes
and see ourselves
together always
in the time
after time.

Next Time We Meet

Let's not keep our clothes on
the next time we meet.
Let's invite a band,
request a drum roll,
take a bow.

We could start with a running jump,
just plunge into each other
like divers in the sea
collecting jewels.

Or we could wait until the hottest day,
slide into each others' nakedness,
slip and slip again
until we sleep rejoicing.

You could wear your hat.
That would be allowed.
And I could keep my
boots on just in case.

Let's not keep our clothes on
the next time we meet.
We'll excuse ourselves
to the company,
explain it as a dare,
or something in the dip,
and giggle up the stairs
without a glance.

Or we could go for a walk
and wave at passers by,

stop at the grocery store
for supplies,
oblivious to everyone's surprise.

Oh no! Let's not keep our clothes on
the next time we meet.
We could take turns
or do it together,
set a record either way.
No need for candles
or violins,
just the hot unzipping sound
of blue jeans
sending forth the whole of us,
peeling away the layers
that falsify the flesh.

Next time we meet!

Man Made Breakfast

This morning my man made breakfast.
He actually cracked a few eggs.
His diploma rocked on its hook
when the toaster popped,
but he kept right on
buttering me up
a piece of rye.

"What a treasure"
a friend admired.
And I thought of diamonds and gold
but never breakfast.

I slipped on my smiling mask
let her echo fill the room.
Was it just my bitch pills
kicking in
or had she come in
a frame too late?
The splattered words
and bloodied love
all soaked up.
What is breakfast anyway
next to the gentle
opening of a heart?

This is the nineties after all.
Are real men only up to
making breakfast?

No Other Road

She is no longer
the black and white photo,
Persephone ripe for plucking,
but somebody's mom,
a budding crone
who dances the rumba
with the love of her life,
who gives her form
and a reason
and will laugh with her until the end.

You were just playmates
in the Elysian Fields.

There never was another road
but the one you forged,
the one that brought you here with me.

Hanging On

I must not see you now,
your body rivaling Greek statues,
your song a cradle lullaby.
You are hidden,
tucked away behind
the heavy velvet curtain
so the brilliance of you
will not dissolve
the sight of me.
With you I will melt away,
form messy puddles,
seep into the crevices and
drip sideways slowly.

I cannot see you now
or my mind will wither
like dry leaves
and whirl about, scattered
and half dead.

The heart of my mother
will betray
the me that is growing
in my own womb,
carry me to oblivion
into the raging void.

I dare not see you now
for fear of drowning
in the sea of "us" and "we".
I would dive right in,
the deeper the better,

and forget in an instant
how to swim.

The touch of your hand
would poison me delirious.
The tears behind your eyes
would taunt my madness open.

I will not see you now,
though you stand before me
waiting.
I am not scolding.
I am not casting you aside.
I am merely hanging on,
breath to breath
against my own death.

Like Breathing

I didn't dream you
long ago
and wait full of faith
for you to arrive

There was no other life before
that brushed our souls together –
an eternal courtship

No sky opened up
No ground trembled

I love you simply -
like a seed loves Earth -
like breathing

Frog Prince

You are a frog.
You may have been born a prince,
but now you are spotted green and wet,
the witches curse,
or your mother's,
but certainly not mine.
I have my own witches to contend with.
I have worked hard
to be a princess.
No magic kiss transformed me,
only walking tenderly
along the sharp side
of the razor of my own life.
When I kiss you
it's because I love you,
Little Green Frog.
Don't go promising
to be a prince for me.
I'm not listening.
I don't believe in magic.
Search for the beautiful princess
inside yourself
and ask her for a kiss.
And then, if you still love me
what wonderful friends we will be.

Woman to Man
(For Eddie)

I am fair from sunless days.
You had olive gold beginnings.
I know the silence of cold night air.
You burn with midday madness.
I move in circles, full to empty to full again.
You are fertile always, steadfast.
I speak in cool white
touching tree tops like the wind.
You race and streak the sky
with all your passions blazing.
I pull in, my dark side hidden.
You boldly grant the world your full array.
I pulse the earth that takes the seed.
You warm the unseen womb.
We rule the sky in separate turns
and wait to join at dusk and dawn.

Feeding the Cat

Winter chill creeping in
and you limping with your cane.
All the years unfold before us
in a single act.
You pick up the bowl
and I scoop out the can.

MOTHERING

Stepmother's Cry
(for Jeremy, age 3)

How do I let go of
the child that reached into my stone
and plucked out the sacred flower;
the child who grasped my hand
and ran against the wind;
the child who called my name
from beyond the darkness
and knew that I would come?

How do I let go of
the child I sang into slumber
and wakened from stormy dreams;
the child whose tears pierced my breast
and planted there his name;
the child whose untamed laughter
echoes in the dusty
corners of my home?

How do I let go of
the scared brown eyes
that begged not to leave again;
the delicate crimson lips
that ask about God and why
and whispered goodbye
with a last brave kiss?

Silhouettes

Alone in bed
I am rocked in
arms of silence

One thin light trickles
from the far end
He is writing

My unborn stirs
I am filled with
the Great Breath

Half Brothers
(for Jeremy, age 10)

He waves his small round hand
at the bus that swallows you again.
For a time he cannot measure
your bike stands quiet in the hall.
He points to your shelf,
pulls at your games,
babbles to your photograph.
He looks in your bed and
you are not there.
He wishes you goodnight
like a prayer.

A guard lets you in.
You ride an elevator
to your door,
eat hot dogs in front of the T.V.
Movie stars hang on your bedroom wall.

You read the same book over again.
Saying goodnight to
your black haired mother
you put yourself to bed.

Cesarean Birth
(For Gabriel)

I wanted to greet you slowly, in whispers,
with cool light and warm water.
Instead I let them squeeze and push you.
My fault they said.
You were big enough to burst, but not quite ready.
You stayed. I held you, breathing the All,
our rhythm still throbbing, strong.

They stuck us with tentacles,
an insect, a telephone pole,
and poisoned us together,
for our "own good."

Lost in foggy fear I disappeared.
They pumped the spasms through me,
telling me to spit you out - a bad taste.

I writhed hour by hour
as they pumped more and more,
counting heartbeats on a screen,
heartbeats even and strong,
rating our pain on a scale,
blaming me.
Blaming me, tied to their bed,
believing their Black Magic
instead of the Mother.

I first saw you in a dream,
cut from my belly like my heart
at the Great Sacrifice.

Covered with my blood
you flashed before me,
cringing at the white and icy assault.
Screaming for my warmth
you were wrapped in cotton.
Longing for our single breath
you were whisked away from me.

Green gowns melted into hallway walls.
I wept as I was wheeled to greet you.
You refused their rubber tits and sugar water,
waited for my breast and sucked strong.
Familiar voices smiled
into our starry silence.
I could not move. I could not cry out.

I begged them not to take you again.
But my words were weak on jailers' ears.
They turned out my lights and closed my door.
Sleep was a handsome paramour.

Your late night cry woke me
to darkness, an empty womb.
Sleep still tugged at my brain
as I recalled the butcher's smile,
the henchman's mask.
Sleep. Sleep reached out a soft hand,
offered to slip me into heaven for awhile.

But you cried
and I called across the hall,
"Bring my baby. My baby!"
You were not a stranger when I held you
and I held you till dawn.

Midweek Vacation

Barely filled midday bus
businessmen and briefcases
young women with braids
grandmothers clutching handbags

The child sits quietly
like all the others
half grown.
In separate seats
who wave goodbye
to fathers
with broad smiles
that fade as eyes glaze
watching long after the bus
rolls out the distance.

Smiling Baby

You were a smiling baby,
wide round infectious smile.
You clung to me like life.
I rocked you long into each night
for slumber took you slowly.

You early left my lap
looking for another climb
a few feet away.
But always you'd return
with more to share
of squeals and dusty hands.
And if, while gone, you'd fall
I'd rush to see.

Now you are a pirate, a cowboy, a soldier
with guns and swords to fight the foe.
I am just the lunch lady,
a juice dispenser with a smile.
You are gone to the Wild West,
another galaxy,
while I stay home and
do your laundry.

But I notice every morning,
with a flicker in my heart,
that you appear beside my bed,
slip in to say hello,
clutch my arm, and
Oh, that magic smile!

Miscarriage I

You are not a
small dark sack
sealed in plastic
to be probed and labeled.

You are more than
tissue and blood
poured into a jar.

You are a soft amulet bag
hung from my heart.
My palms cradle you
around my still
round belly.

I feel you flutter
somewhere in the night
and set you free.

Miscarriage II

Switch turned off
the living room suddenly empty

A shattered teacup
swept away

A whole sunny afternoon
on the porch with blank pages

The white wicker chair
stops rocking in the wind

No key on the hook now
and the spare missing too

The undialed telephone
hangs quiet on the wall

The basketful of mending
will always be

For Mother

I cradle the little goosedown head
of your granddaughter
and feel myself flow
as she sucks sweetly at my breast.
In a prayerful pause
I see her deep blue eyes,
with the depth of an angel's gaze,
watching mine, mirroring me.

In the moment of a heartbeat
I fall back through time
to the other side
looking up at you.

Filled with your wordless hum
I feel the heat of
the Great Fire
fierce between us.

All That's Left

I used to bake bread.
My muffins were supreme.
I imagined that someday
I'd make them for you,
running home from school
breathlessly chattering.

And the garden out back
would flow over 'til leaves fell.
Then we'd sit by the fire.
I would teach you to draw
or to weave and to dream.

But the garden lies fallow now,
the muffins have no tins
and you go to the sitter after school.
I am not twenty or thirty.

She is gone now like the muffins,
eaten all up.
All that's left is the dreaming
and you are teaching me how.

How Do I Hold You Now?

How do I hold you now?
I used to be close by
to catch you.
But then the bumps were small
the falls an inch or two.

There used to be rails on your bed,
locks on the cabinet doors.
I used to know how to hold you.

I can turn off the T.V.
send the bully home.
But you still have nightmares
and a brother who's gone
and I can't explain.

How do I hold you now
against your sense of rage in me,
against my unspoken tears
and the loneliness?

I look at your soft pale face,
your wondering eyes.
How do I hold you now?

Water
(For My Daughter Sappho)

Cool faucet water fills my two cupped hands
My little girl leans over the sink to sip
I look at the curls of her hair
auburn and wild like my own
Suddenly, I am at the Well
pulling up from the deep
We are at the edge of the Great Lake
We have been stooping on the River's edge
together
since the beginning of time
The water is silver wisdom
She drinks slowly from my palms

The Letter

Screaming baby at 3 am, teeth just beginning to
show, sore nipples, another nasty diaper.

Husband wincing, groaning twisting all night,
moaning "more juice,"
the doctors asking when and where but not telling
why.

Hot toast and coffee both gone cold
dishes left on the table
dirty clothes spilling from the basket
another day of rain and rain

A boy nagging to play checkers again,
his wet jacket dropped in the hall,
karate kicks to the refrigerator door.

Finally Friday afternoon
a small white envelope in the box
hello from a sister
who has just planted daffodils
pulled up the last pumpkins
gazed out at snowy mountains

Reading the letter again...
she phones for a pizza,
the groceries still in their bags.
Big Bird blaring, she sits at her desk -
notebook and purple pen -
and writes and writes and writes

Metaphor for Mothering

Sea storms sneak up swiftly
take us off guard.
I cannot swim or
float to shore
with you grabbing on.
I must push
against the undertow
keep from tumbling
while you writhe in my arms
screaming "Mommie! Mommie!"
I walk in slow motion
as the waves break over us
my best instinct
to hold you up into safety
as long as I can.

WAR

Wave: A Memoir

My father was a regular G.I. He and his fellow troops issued supplies to the European front and followed behind combat troops, always trailing through the destruction after the battle, but never being aimed at, never firing back. Finally, Europe was liberated. Japan was the next front. My father, like so many others, was ordered to invade that beautiful land. He was sent there as a combatant. He was sent there to kill and perhaps be killed. After a few months in the Philippines he was on shipboard with the other soldiers, crowded and lonely for home.

They were all terrified of what waited ahead, invading enemy territory, a Pacific island they had never seen before. Europe had been vaguely familiar, reminiscent of home. But, Japan was another world, and the Japanese soldier a foreboding and unknown entity. My father, like many of his counterparts, kept his deepest fears inside. If he had dared let himself fully feel his own terror, he would have been lost to himself, given over to that other sphere where nothing makes sense anymore. The die had been cast. He was on his way. He was in the hands of fate now. All he could do was hold fast to hope.

One day flowed into the next. Playing cards, smoking cigarettes, talking about girlfriends waiting back home and the job or house they'd have someday; anything to keep from feeling where they were going, what they were doing, what lay ahead. And truly they did not know what lay ahead. How could anyone? Beyond imagining. Beyond all human comprehension.

And then the news... A radio dispatch... A bomb, the biggest, was breaking down the enemy. There was cheering and laughter and hope that the end was near, that their dreams of home would really come true. They could pick up where they had left off, and life, their lives, would go on as planned. Now they glued themselves to the radio listening for updates, making bets, making promises to God. Finally, it came, three days later, another bomb, another city, Japan had surrendered. Relief raced through every muscle. My father breathed his deepest breath. The war was over. He had been spared.

The ship came alive. Music could be heard in the mess hall. Nervous laughter was everywhere. My father wrote letters home, one to his mother with facts and reassurance, one to his sweetheart with love and dreams. He imagined a few more months of that drab green and army rations, then the boat ride home. A few more months of jeeps and guns and he'd put it all behind him. He still didn't know what none of them knew, the price they had paid. With the end in sight anything seemed bearable. Anything *seemed* bearable.

He didn't feel the shock waves then. They were imperceptible, distorted, clouded by the unreality of victory. And when he saw, his mouth agape, the ravaged earth, the rubbled city, the people gone for miles around, he still didn't know that he was changed forever. There was no going home again, home to innocence or home to glory. No one will ever be home that way again.

My father didn't talk much about those times, and most people who knew him never knew his story. He wept when he told me of those days, not only for what he saw, but for what cannot be seen. His life was spared, and thousands more, but he was never sure it was an even trade.

He didn't know me then, riding through those leveled streets, silently taking in the smoke and stench that filled the air. He had not even dreamed me as he watched the children shuffling through the wreckage for something familiar to hang on to. He couldn't imagine then that what he saw was only the beginning of a wave so great that I would feel it too someday, that all of us would feel it deep in our marrow forever.

My father went on to have a good life. He was a gentle man who always felt blessed. He died recently in a memory care facility. Surprisingly, in his final days, although he no longer remembered my mother, he began telling anyone who would listen that he had been in Hiroshima after the bomb dropped. That event became the central focus of his identity when most of who he was otherwise had left him, and as he faced his own death.

My father was very happy having a family, grandchildren and great grandchildren. But he never lost sight of the wave, the human evil that always lurked. And in his quiet moments when he looked out over the ocean he felt sad and shameful and angry about the human capacity for such savagery. And I believe he knew, though he never said it out loud, that since that time we have all been existentially searching, like children through the wreckage, for something safe to hang on to.

Waiting For War
(March 2003)

There is a hyacinth growing
in my bedroom,
found by chance,
left behind last Fall,
in a shadowed basement corner,
like a frightened refugee
welcomed back to the light.

I was scrounging for some soil
and a little pot
to start Spring seeds in
and a molly screw
because it holds tight…
and some glue.

After three months of deep freeze,
frightened stiff, pacing like prisoners,
the future unclear,
we sat this afternoon
out back on the porch,
melting snow still two feet high,
the paths we laid so long ago
buried now,
like hope is sometimes.

We held our hands up
against the sun,
shielding our eyes from blinding,
wishing we could hold it all back,
the Call to War,

helpless and heavy we wait,
resigned to the end despite our wanting.

Still, there is a hyacinth
blooming inside.
And the only true thing to believe in
is that I love you.

Sentry
(Dedicated to military veterans everywhere)

I look into your soft eyes
as you hold up your tattered shield –
to keep me from seeing …
The Beast
fangs dripping…
and you with nowhere to run.

But I am a grown woman.
I can only feel your story
like a distant mist,
a dream I can only glimpse in pieces.

But don't think I can't hear
the desperate howl behind your silence,
the crashing of your heart on the jungle floor.

It is you I really want to see,
even when it hurts.

I know there is safety in the Inside Place,
when there is no more "ollie ollie ins-free,"
and the wound and the growl
are deeper than Earth.

I ache to hold your broken heart,
and sing and rock and rest.
But I know the power of that Inside Place
to hide you away forever.

So I keep vigil outside your door,
three feathers in my hair,
beating my woman round drum,
humming the ancient Warrior Song …
all night long.

Sisters of the Jungle, of the Desert Sands
(Dedicated to all women who love a veteran)

Around any corner
a moment to moment ambush awaits,
a sound or a smell,
a child's cry, a nighttime caress.

You wait with a Warrior's heart,
though the battles never cease,
ready to embrace the demon once again.

You are ready
but never prepared.

You more than understand.
You ache with comprehension.
You are mad and writhe
with the awful knowledge of war.

You have tasted it.
You have felt its knife blade at your throat,
heard it crashing on the kitchen floor.
It rips at the fiber of your sensibilities
like hail, like fire.

You don a shield
welded with the grit of your own true heart,
your greatest weapon, loyalty.
I hear a howl in your silent tears,
a sacred text in your unspoken words.

You are the true battle buddy,
no bayonet or boots,
just your utter belief in the mission -
in your man.

So Deep
(Written for the wives of troops and veterans)

Don't think I don't know
how wounded you are
So deep my love
my heart drips with your sorrow

But you can't see me
You have built a fortress
to protect me from the enemy –
the dark inside of humanity –
and stand guard as if you think
I would wail and run from the Beast
hide under the bed like a child

You can't see me
my heart half gone with grieving
But I have armor too
shields and swords and the will to live

So deep my love
I can face your enemy down

A fire burns in me that
your bricks and mortar cannot put out

If you could glimpse me
only for a moment
you would know
I can walk through fire too
charred dead bodies
piles of bone and blood

don't think I don't know them
So deep my love

LOSS

Letting Go of Charlie
(A Hospice Farewell)

You are not just another name on a list.
You are more than a pile of papers
lined up in the drawer.
My pen stumbles as I write the last report,
no room on the final form for the life you lived,
for the young soldier home from the war,
the father, the gardener, the carpenter,
the story teller.
No box that says" friend."
Nothing to tell of those
whose lives you blessed
over and over again.
My throat grows tight and the questions blur
as I circle the simple answers
that do not tell of the love and the loyalty
and the loss.
Goodbye, dear man.
Goodbye.

Fire

A room in my keeping
as old as my grandpa
where my children often played
and the piano sang
and we said prayers together

Now a damp pile
broken glass
charred beams
burnt paper off the walls
here and there a piece of unmarred molding

Only a corner really
but dead and buried
turned in an instant
to skeleton and bone

The wound screams out at me
a warning in the wind
blows from its gaping mouth
and all I can do is stare

Grace

Buried in a morning snow
by sleeping earth
that took her like a seed.

Barren days crept in
to cover up the grave
and icy winds
stopped carrying her name.

Yet still in spring
her sweet daffodils.

Leaves

Flat dishwater after breakfast,
a late August sun
lazy on the sill.
I recall this blue and gold mug,
back six,
no, eight years.
I packed it
in an old wine box
with other delicate glass,
wrapped it away in dusty newsprint
with the friends I'd leave behind.
I was twenty five and wished
the moving on would end.

Leaves entwined in tiny jars
tumble over the sill.
Time to plant
before the Autumn chill.

Mourning Mom
(A Love Story for Eddie)

You run around me
placing candles and incense
while I sit listening to the cellos sing
my mournful heart trickling it's hot liquid
through all of me.

You bring me shawls and pillows
so I can curl up
a babe once more
sad and scared that
Mommy's far away.

The two year old will not allow it
will stamp and cry and holler "No!"
and you will bring her tea in her favorite cup
and remind her that she is me
grown and whole and a mother myself.

You fix a little snack for us.
Spacey bells ringing a dreamy tune
as I contemplate eternal nothingness
surrender and return
the Grand Reunion with it all.

You dry my tears, take me by the hand
and lead me to my own warm bed
you so alive - so close it hurts.
And I know that all of this is practice
for someday letting go of you.

Forever
(For Mom)

Bigger than the Himalayas
it plunges out to infinity.
I may explode
from the agony of missing her.
I feel it in my essence,
in the core of me.
Like labor, the pain so great,
or a limb torn away.

How do I wrench from my being
the One, my oldest home,
whatever pains between us
faded into the hills?
It is a Primal Longing,
a Ritual Sacrifice.
I am forever changed,
and Forever is a bitter root.

But, as I once lived in her
she still lives in me.

For An Instant
(For Mom)

This song -
a simple tune
over and over
while I drove
back and forth

She was alive then
soft hands
and sweet smell

Now, for an instant…
the song…
and she still is

Father

Look, the zinnias have opened
And he died just yesterday

Now a goldfinch sings
Its mate responds from afar
He takes flight

Forsythia

I am slipping past my life
I glimpse it now and then
in the dusty corner at my desk
at the bookcase browsing.
But mostly the phone is ringing
the laundry piling.
Captured by the dark cloud
of my own mother's emptiness
I chase clutter from room to room.
Out of breath and aching
I am pushed back endlessly
by the tides of her discontent.

I am slipping past my life
the way I slide by
forsythia in spring.
Their tiny yellow stars
begin to fall
before I see them
and once again I missed their call.

Total Eclipse of Jean

The computer we shared
has our files…saved together –
Such sad intimacy-
gone unnoticed for what it is…till now.

I naturally imagine her closet at home,
her favorite things hanging still,
some unique, some silly, some just "Jean."
Oh, mournful intimacy!

I sit in the chair she used to use,
listening to people she once knew.

How it pains… this intimacy.

When I open a drawer
her name peers out on unused little cards
that only I see.
I cannot yet let them go.

Funny, she was there when I was not
and the other way around,
mirror images, both
raised with sputnik and the Beatles
and the Viet Nam War.

Oh, sadness!

Where are her keys to "our room" door?
In what pocket or handbag?
Who dares to look so close to really see?

I talk with the others,
hushed in lunchroom lines
and sometimes smile…remembering.

She is everywhere in her absence,
her name gone from the door,
her bookcase empty,
the message machine changed.

I cannot believe …
Over and over again
it wells up anew
and I gasp. Not Jean!

I am inside myself these days
wondering, imagining
how a woman her age faces death,
how I will someday.

Tonight I am savoring the shadow and the light
of a springtime eclipse
as she would wish for me,
feeling her in the air around me
as I make soup, sew on a button,
stare long out my window at the night.

SPIRIT

God

I cannot lose sight of you
even in the olive pit
your ancient tendrils
knot and swirl

You burn eternal in the fire
timeless in the air I breathe

There are some who say
it is not in me to know you
but they mean you in your disguise-
your magical arrivals
with glitter and brass bands
 not your gentle nudging
in my dreams
or in the rich soil when I dig in my garden-
our garden, yours and mine
the one where I place the seeds
and you do all the rest.

I cannot lose sight of you,
 not even with my eyes closed

Divinity

Under the ragged maple tree

I see it

In the playful light
That filters through the feverfew
Surrounding me

I see it

In the charcoal as I draw
In the paper I write upon
The keys of the old piano
Photos of those now gone.

I see it here and more

The swing swaying in the dark
And the crackle of the fire

Like Birds Singing

O, to rise every day
and let go a miracle
without notice or applause
without awe
but simply because
the song is inside
pressing
and nothing else will do.

Divine Puttering

What better use than puttering
for potting tendrils from the sill,
setting out those precious roots
against all possibility
with faith that they will grow?

What better use than puttering
for touching God?

Singing

The song starts
far below my heart
long before time
in the core
Earth's eternal rhyme

It rises slowly
like the moon
like the smoke of the sacrificial fire
past all the broken places
and memory
and fills me like love

It vibrates the vessel
as it seeks the light
of the only way out
up, up
like the first green shoots
breaking ground in spring
until at last it is home
the tender notes
soaring toward heaven

Awe

*(For Thay Quang Duc – Vietnamese Buddhist monk
who immolated himself to protest the oppression
of Buddhists in 1963)*

Black and white photo
Burning
The chanting monk captures my breath
I sweat and sweat
feel my insides deep
seeping out
How does a man sit still
flames tearing him away
calmly singing

How dare I claim
to pray
to sacrifice
to mean anything at all.

Soul Awakening
(For the island of Poros)

It's not the handshakes
Or the early morning smiles
Not the mountains or the sea
Hillside shanties or olive trees
Not the ferry all day long
The bouzouki player's song -
Bigger than all of these
A simple place to breathe
Where my weary soul belongs

Mother, Is That You?

Just when I said, "Yes!"
The buzzing, growling flutter of hummingbird –
Over and over she came.
I chose to see her as a sign –

Mother, is that you?

From there to our first look at the farmhouse –
Both in awe, both home at last.
Now wild daisies grace our yard.
I always wanted wild daisies.

Mother is that you?

Marble Mountain
(Viet Nam 2003)

Out of the darkness
Carved in the cool cave wall
Quan Yin lights my way

Buddha Madonna
A song echoes from your cave.
Is it you or me?

Sitting in Maura's Kitchen

Sitting in Maura's kitchen
alone,
touching the blue flowered tablecloth,
I remember her bright eyes.
I see her hands,
wrinkling like my own,
arranging a candle,
a bouquet of sage
in perfect places
as simple as a glance.

She doesn't plan or figure,
she just unfolds
in brilliant colors.
She finds earth and sky in everything,
makes a treasure box
of any shelf or bowl.
A scarf adorns her mirror,
a purple waterfall,

a painted bead on her windowsill
the eye of God.

Birds fly on her spice tins,
fish swim across her plates,
hats with feathers or without
hang in corners
like the plants that grow
everywhere she goes.
A little piece of me
grows here too
sitting in Maura's kitchen, alone.

I feel my colors glow,
reflecting, catching fire.

Perhaps I am the bird.
Perhaps I am the eye of God.

Delphi

Below the cliff
above the abyss
in a crevice of the Mother
around a mountain bend
it looms for all to see with unbelieving eyes.

Columns and temple
chiseled with skill and longing
strewn in ruin
along the Sacred Way.
Friezes of horses and heroes
statues of soldiers and sphinx -
rubbled remains
of long ago pilgrims
who came from afar
by mule and cart
on foot and on cane
searching for God and destiny.

We come still
now in buses and cars
with chattering French children
seeking photos
and curious Japanese
who are called unknowing
to this sacred cradle
to wander and wonder among themselves.

Yet loudest of all are the birds
singing a welcome to morning light
and dew drops on the pines.
Hawks float in circles

above the highest cliff
searching into crannies and
back around again,
guardians, watching, waiting, reminding.

When the gates are closed and people gone
all that has ever been
is the mountain -
the temple but a landslide.

All that is alive
since the beginning of time
all that is God
all that we need -
the mountains of Delphi.

Blanket Weaver

Your swift steady fingers
carefully select
the colors of my life.

Give the pattern a full array
to cover all the distances
and sorrow.

Make some strands thick and strong,
the bonds of time and circumstance,
and others just a thread
where lovers part.

Save the smoothest
for the edges
where unraveling hurts most.

Keep the pattern uneven
with room enough to laugh,
and keep it simple
for every flaw to show.

Weave it tight for strength
and extra warmth.
Fold in loose ends.

Then decorate the edges
with unwoven strands,
all the choices left unmade.

Mostly make it
long enough to grow in
and wide enough to share.

My Church

My church today -
arms outstretched,
the open sky
a fair wind fluttering my face –

I was blessed there
among the congregation -
birch and pine,
maple and ash,
chestnut and cherry.

I melded with the Earth
and floated also in the sky,
Big and All, was I,
and wide,
all of me
swirling in
the melody of spirits -
dancing on the edge of Grace.

MEDITATION ON TREES

I am sitting at my desk watching the trees change colors. There is still a variegation of green mixed in with the reds, oranges and yellows as dusk peers up from the horizon. I wonder how young I was when I first noticed that the seasons ebb and flow and when I first felt the grace of these majestic cycles.

Like the seasons, writing comes to me in cycles. A summer harvest of images ideas and sound, and then the ground lies cold and unyielding for a time while the unseen germinates, gathers the magic and suddenly sprouts anew.

Now the wind blows and I see the dancing of leaves and branches all in harmony. I heard once that some people can tell the kind of tree by the sound the leaves make when the wind rushes through them. What sort of life does a person live who is the companion of trees? How different a life from mine? In truth though, I have learned about the changing sounds of those I love. A sentence or a look from their eyes and I know what the thought is, what the need.

With people there is a necessity, a dependence. I learned to read my mother, to anticipate. It felt like loyalty. With my children it is different. I read them because they are of me, of my heart and womb. We were once one. I want to know who they are and what they need.

I see that when the branches bend, the grasses bend as well. The wind is not particular, no prejudice or favorites. We're all in this together, the field might say. And so they are, so we are. No single disconnected act. We all move together in the invisible dance. I wish I could look down from way above and see the grand waltz the way we see drawings in fields, watch the two step from on high.

Nothing could be as grand as trees in autumn. They have color like people have personalities. Funny, or maybe telling, how leaves start out in some hue of green, the conformity of youth and insecurity. As summer pushes on we see them straining, bulging out their fullest proudly. Then a chill spikes the air. They all get a little tipsy and wind down. The fruit begins to fall with over-ripeness. One by one they seem to grasp the end with grace. With nothing left to risk, they show themselves in full array. This is really who I am, they seem to say. That is how it is with trees. Courage and wisdom in the end.

I remember my mother telling me that a woman her age shouldn't wear her hair long. It wasn't proper. I don't remember her ever stopping to watch the trees change color in the fall. She lived with my father in that house for thirty-three years. They were rooted. Being rooted is passive, something that just happens from staying in one place too long. Having roots is active, a way of life, that keeps us centered, gives us purpose no matter where we are.

I understand that trees have roots that grow as deep as the tree is tall and as wide as the branches. A mirror image down below, hidden from view, without all the fanfare and glory. Just the simple steady growing deeper with time. Those are the roots I want, as deep and as wide as I need them to be, to steadfastly balance me. I want my roots to be the unadorned inward delving that furrows a way to my soul.

Winter trees are also marvelous. The Grand Sleep feigns their death, earth's skeletons stark and gray. And yet a great mystery stirs in them. They are resting, gathering in to replenish and renew. Their summer vigor needs their winter repose. Power comes from gathering in, to ourselves and our own stillness, from reaching down into the core of our existence for sustenance.

Trees do not need to be beautiful always, to be noticed or applauded or needed. They simply let go when it's time to, take care of themselves in their own natural rhythm. How much healthier I would be if I lived more like a tree. How wonderful and freeing it would be if we could all accept quiet times of life, if we could each take ourselves that seriously. "No, I can't. I'm in my quiet time."

I once spent a day lying in the woods alone, asking the natural world for messages that I could live by. As I looked up I saw the surrounding trees converge high above me. Their limbs and branches were all entwined, so that I could not make out one from the other. There were many varieties, young and old, thick and slender. And there were smaller ones stretching their way up, searching for available sunlight.

Suddenly, I felt myself in the midst of a true community. These trees had come together, not by choice, but by circumstances. Their planting and rooting there was by chance, not unlike our own. They thrived, sharing resources with the others that destiny had placed by their sides. The older and stronger ones had more, the younger and smaller ones had less. But eventually, the older ones would die off and leave room and sunlight for smaller ones to grow.

There was a Grand Harmony about these woods, something eternal and right. No one tree or species could claim it all. They stood together with different needs and separate gifts, limbs woven like fingers in prayer, a great web of necessity and reliance, of practicality and holiness.

When I left the woods, I headed down the hill to join an encampment of friends. I could see from above all the different colors of their clothing, the reds, oranges and greens. Some were laughing, some were working, some were sitting still. And I could see, beyond my tears of delight, the Grand Harmony in them too.

I can still see it now and then, when it swells up out of the chaos of everyday demands. I listen to children squabbling, and the phone ringing while I am cooking dinner. Suddenly, I remember those woods and smile. Now, though daylight is fading, I feel moved to go outside, stand in the brilliant field and make a long low bow for all of us to our lovely companions, the trees.

ABOUT THE AUTHOR

Kate Dahlstedt's poetry has appeared in *Mildred*, *Modern Haiku*, *Pilgrimage*, *Voices* and other publications. Her essay, "Meditation on Trees," was first published in *Pilgrimage*: *Reflections on the Human Journey* vol. 24, number 4. She has also authored professional book chapters and journal articles.

As a psychotherapist with over 35 years of clinical experience, Kate's work has taken her to the rice paddies of Vietnam with U.S. veterans, the mountains of Greece with spiritual seekers, and the townships of South Africa working with AIDS victims. Some of her poetry has been translated into Greek and Vietnamese and read at national and international events.

Kate and her husband Ed Tick co-founded the Hudson Valley Writers Guild in 1982. They co-founded and directed Soldier's Heart, Inc., a non-profit addressing the invisible wounds of war, from 2006-2019.

Kate is a mother, stepmother, grandmother and godmother. In addition to her private practice, she now puts her creative energy into gardening, writing, renovating the 1850 farmhouse she shares with her husband in central Massachusetts, and being "Grammy."

ACKNOWLEDGMENTS

Pete and Sophie Rogers have not only cheered this project on, they have given me the gift of feedback, friendship and a generous donation to make this publication a reality. Thank you. I love you.

Valerie Legeay has been a fellow traveler with me in many realms. I am grateful for her undying encouragement and support for this book, and hope this publication will put her at ease.

Jennifer Leigh Selig has provided me with the publishing assistance that I never dreamed possible. My gratitude is overwhelming.

Ed Dahlstedt, my father, gave me my first book of poetry and knew I had it in me.

Ed Tick, supporter extraordinaire for the many years of living these works with me and providing final guidance and editing as well as occasional fruit smoothies for sustenance and soothing.